THE DIVINE
Human

A Contemplative Journey Through Poetry and Art

GENNY GENEVICH

Balboa Press books may be ordered through booksellers or by contacting:

Balboa Press
A Division of Hay House
1663 Liberty Drive
Bloomington, IN 47403
www.balboapress.com
1 (877) 407-4847

ISBN: 978-1-5043-5005-1 (sc)
ISBN: 978-1-5043-5006-8 (e)

Library of Congress Control Number: 2016901570

Print information available on the last page.

Balboa Press rev. date: 03/31/2016

BALBOA.
PRESS
A DIVISION OF HAY HOUSE

ABOUT THE FRONT COVER

The practice of meditation is thousands of years old spanning across the globe with a myriad of meanings and approaches to its practice.

This solitary figure on the front cover symbolizes states of contemplation, reflection, and introspection – inner pathways of transformation that lead into a deepening Silence wherein our divine essence may be realized – and become, through our individual and collective consciousness, the evolutionary rebirth of humanity.

DEDICATION

This book is dedicated to

SUZANNE FAGEOL

*in gratitude for her profound guidance
throughout my years of deepening into the awakening process.*

With love,

CONTENTS

POETRY AND ART:
THE CONTEMPLATIVE JOURNEY

ACKNOWLEDGEMENTS

To each of you, I bow in gratitude for your imprint upon this work. *"It takes a village …"*

Deborah Koff-Chapin: Founder of Touch Drawing and author of *Soul Cards* who was always available for professional advice and support. Thank you, Deborah.

Barbara Marx Hubbard: Futurist, Author, and Pioneer in the field of Conscious Evolution who encouraged me to pursue publication. Thank you, Barbara.

Julie Marino: a dear friend who walked the way with me from the first poem to the completion of the book. Thank you, Julie.

Anne Bosch: a generous soul who often gave of her time to critique the work and offer continuous support. Thank you, Anne.

To Spirit's wind beneath my sails - **the Mystics, Prophets, and Ancestors** - from diverse cultures and spiritual beliefs who deeply influenced my life: **Rumi, Hafiz, Lao Tsu, Sri Aurobindo, Teilhard de Chardin, Thomas Merton, Hildegard, and countless others**. Thank you.

To the authors and teachers of more recent times: **Eckhart Tolle, Caroline Myss, Andrew Harvey, Buddhist/Zen writers, and many others** to whom I owe a debt of gratitude. Thank you.

To **Matthew Smith**, Owner of *The Starving Artist* store in Hendersonville, NC and a Graphic Design Artist who photographed my original drawings for this work. Thank you, Matt.

To **the staff of Balboa Press**, the Self-Publishing Division of its guiding star, *Hay House Publishing,* for your multi-faceted services that shaped this work into its final form. Your professional competence is appreciated … and I thank you.

INTRODUCTION

"You must give birth to your images.
They are the future waiting to be born.
Fear not the strangeness you feel.
The future must enter you long before it happens.
Just wait for the birth,
for the hour of the new clarity."
Rainer Maria Rilke

These words of Rilke, in retrospect, have been the foundation for this unexpected work.

Years ago, I embarked on a spiritual journey through a "desert landscape" tending to increased periods of stillness, silence, and solitude while living an active life. There has been no singular path; I dug deep into the many wells of the One River – Native Americanism, Hinduism, Sufism, Buddhism, Christianity, and others along with a more recent entry into Cosmogenesis and Conscious Evolution.

Early on, while studying the writings of Sri Aurobindo, a world renowned sage from India, I sensed a deep "knowing" from within of a future humanity – and that our evolving human nature is, *in its totality*, Divine. Aurobindo's work bridged the gap between life and spirit as he realized "the highest spiritual reality must be brought down to transform earthly existence and express *through life* the Divine Truth locked in matter." Sri Aurobindo called to the depths of my own soul – a Call that subtly and slowly, without my knowledge of its form, prepared "the future waiting to be born."

At a holistic Conference in Mexico (1996), a professional Soul Reader informally said to me: "You are a poet." Since I had no inclination toward poetry, I paid no attention to her words. However, several months later in a vivid dream, I was presented with a "Certificate for Writing." A seal on the Certificate revealed a picture of the German mystic and visionary, Hildegard of Bingen. Her presence was reassuring: in his book, *Illuminations of Hildegard of Bingen*, Matthew Fox portrays Hildegard "celebrating humanity's divinization … and the immense dignity that goes with it."

Following this dream, seven years passed before the first poem was written, and it came about suddenly without any thought of the Soul Reader's prophecy years earlier. As words formed into sacred poems, they expressed what I was "seeing" and "sensing" of humanity's divinity and led me deeper into that desert landscape. David Jasper, who authored *The Sacred Desert*, states: "Poetry is part of the fabric of the desert, as much a part as sand and rock." For me, the word and the desert became an inseparable Silence, each birthing the other.

Although the final poem was written in 2010, it would be four more years before feeling another tug at the Co-creative heartstrings – this time an inner prodding to enhance each poem with its own "touch drawing" (see Glossary). As Fate would have it, I did attend a Touch Drawing Workshop in the past without any artistic intent. This new creative urge found me renewing the Touch Drawing process and teaching myself how to work with pastel chalks and other techniques.

As the "drawing out" of each poem progressed, spirit faces appeared in the drawings that were not consciously drawn, and frequently, drawings revealed meanings that came about in complete surprise. One such example was drawing the poem, *Beyond Detachment*. I felt a strong and persistent urge to draw the Buddha and surround him in a diamond-shaped frame. After doing so, I suddenly recalled the name of a Buddhist text: "The Diamond Sutra". When I researched its meaning, varied sources described the text as emphasizing *the practice of nonattachment*! Each drawing and its poem held similar experiences and confirmed for me the Divine Presence being the Muse who so patiently guided my soul throughout her lengthy and laborious work. It is this Presence that ultimately IS the poetry and the art … and the Silent Voice living here on earth as *The Divine Human*.

May you embrace your own contemplative journey through this poetry and art.

"Fear not the strangeness you feel …
Just wait for the birth,
For the hour of the new clarity."

Namaste,

Jenny

THE CONTEMPLATIVE JOURNEY

HUMANITY'S DIVINITY

Innate
"of the essence",
"belonging to",
"inherent".

Nothing to bring in,
everything to uncover!

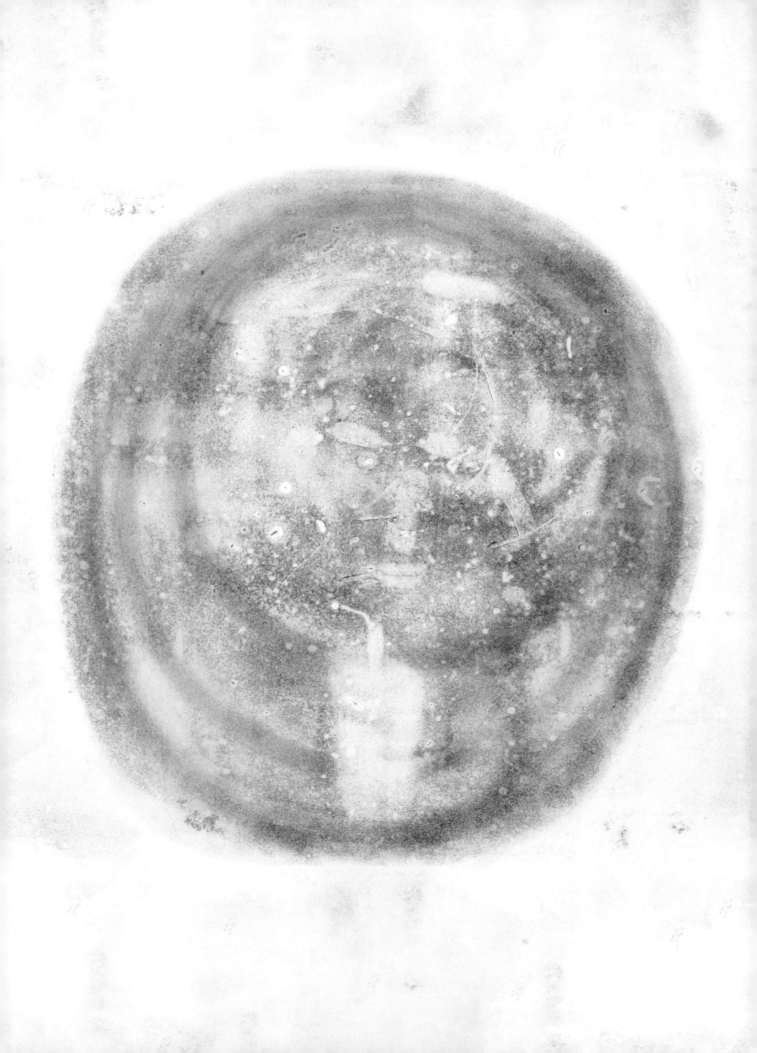

BREATH OF SPIRIT

Since the beginning…

We are breathing the breath of Spirit,
a sacred breath that sustains us
earthly and eternally.
In this breath, we breathe in
all the breath of Creation
that breathes out.

Humanity's breathing breath;
a pulsating, life-giving
rhythm of air
that seeks, without thought,
the next breath of Spirit
to sustain its own breath!

HOLY MIRRORS

All is within this incarnate space,
a vastness so beyond its confines
housing the eternal infinitudes
in rusted caverns of finite flesh.

No separateness echoes
within these chambers of grace,
where all Existence secretly plays
as sitting silence unveils its truths.

A Christ, a Buddha, a Tara,
the sun, and moon, and stars;
holy mirrors in residence
within this incarnate space!

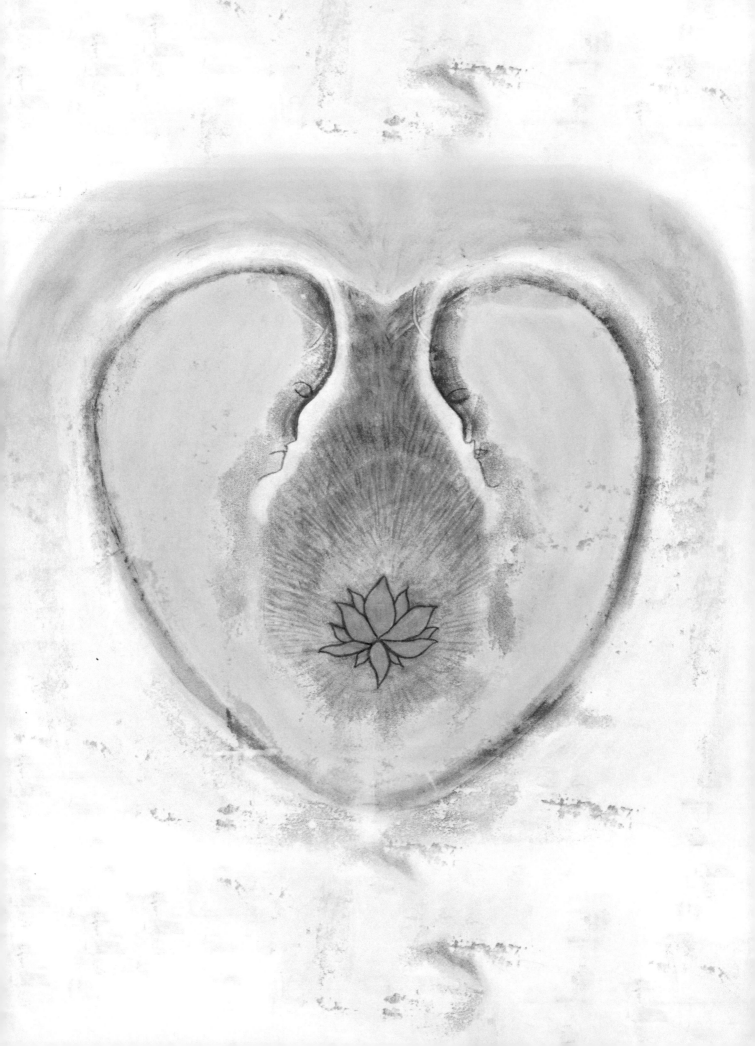

UNFORMED BEAUTY

How breath-taking
this unformed Beauty!
Awaiting her arising
from the deepening places and spaces
of man's divine emptiness.

So dormant she lays,
this unsuspected brilliance of grace!
Gracing to perfection
the void, the silence,
the solitude, the wilderness.

What beckoning power she voices,
in the vastness of these planes!
Calling forth
from fallen ash,
her Phoenix to arise in form.

How breath-taking
this unformed Beauty!
Awaiting her arising
from the deepening places and spaces
of man's divine emptiness!

LANGUAGE OF THE SOUL

The language of the soul speaks unheard
amidst incessant waves of clamoring chatter
as its whisperings fade fast
among the falsities of man's mad busyness.

Humanity's ignorance, once excused,
transforms in the light of Consciousness
through this language of the soul:
Silence.

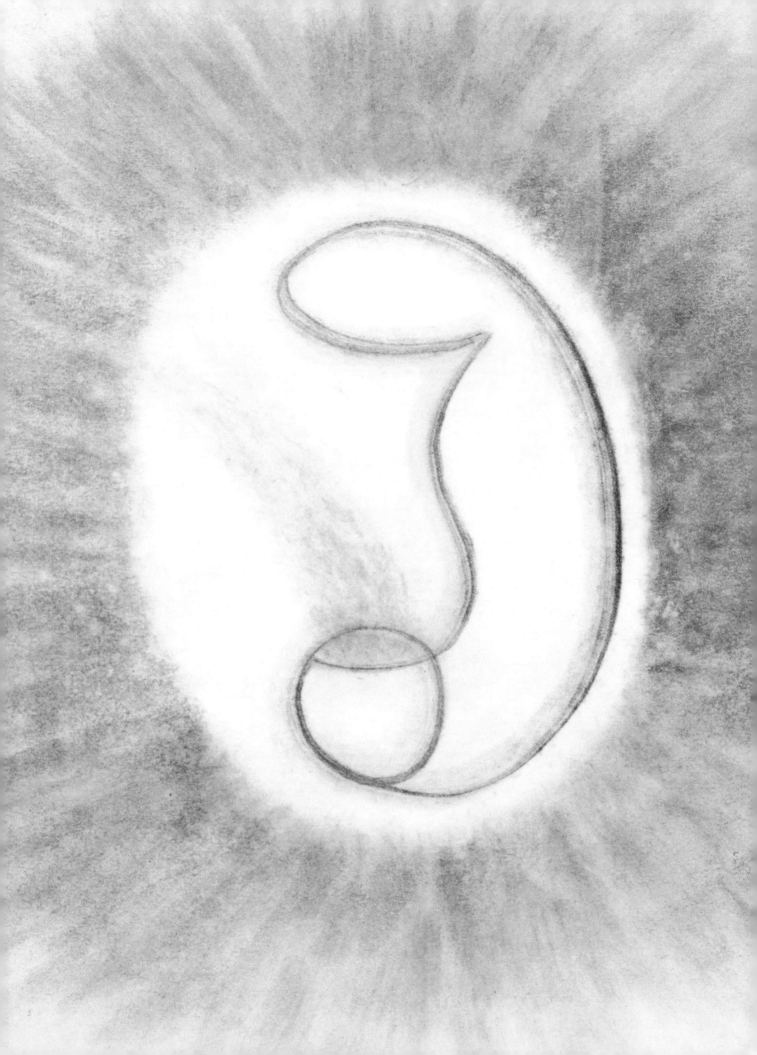

DESERT YEARNINGS

A relentless pursuit
calling, inviting,
saturating
the restless soul.

How sweet the sound of stillness
as silence and solitude
traverse this sanded land,
uprooting bits of stubborn clingings
that so entrain the heart of man.

Across these scapes of mystical terrain
there lures an echo from Rabia's* abode:
"Here she found God,
through an absolute emptiness
impossible to describe."

Desert yearnings…
the Beloved's forerunners
offered in secret to
the restless soul.

* Mystic of Islam

INCARNATE FLESH

All takes place here
within this incarnate flesh!
An embodied meeting place for
matter and Spirit,
earth and heaven,
yin and yang,
war and peace,
birth and death.
A home housing the play of opposites
yet innately embarked on a journey
"toward the One".

Such mystery enshrined
in this incarnate flesh,
host of the human and Divine!
A sacred, holy temple of earth
reflecting an enlightened emptiness
seeks to merge
the living paradox within:
I am
the incarnate flesh
of the
"I AM".

AWAITING AWAKENING

"All this you shall do and more."
(Jesus)

The Source and the powers
lay deep within,
not above in the heavens
nor in some other angelic beings
in another realm.
They lay dormant in our own divine nature,
seeded in the depths of our living soul
and encoded in the structure of our DNA,
awaiting awakening
while here on earth and in this body!

"All this we shall do and more."

BONDAGE

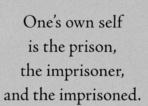

One's own self
is the prison,
the imprisoner,
and the imprisoned.

Until one frees
one's own self,
- and Spirit -
one is bound.

Love
releases the bondage.

SHAPESHIFTER

I must shift my shape while here on Earth
and mold into the visible vastness of Reality:

Creation
The Universe
Divinity
Eternalness
Love

This is what IS!

My vision must be this,
my truth must be this,
my life must be this…

I am *This*!

THIRST FOR THE GRAIL

Insatiable thirst
unquenched.
Subtle longings
unidentified.
Fulfilled desires
unfulfilling.

A darkening restlessness
in pursuit,
answers sought.

Questing on the outside
fearful to search
on the inside.

Paths trodden,
cups drunk,
unquenchable.

Questioning on the outside
leading to search
on the inside.

Fateful ignorance surfacing,
flesh-colored veils lifting,
darkening lightening.

Quiet on the outside
relentlessly questing
on the inside.

Vision sighted,
thirst quenching!

CRUCIFIXION

"It is finished."
Scripture

Past,
over,
forgiven,
complete.

My blood, My life
compassionately offered
so that you may see and walk the Earth
beyond your suffering ways.

Don't stay stuck on the cross,
learn of its teachings
for it has much to say…
then move on, transform, resurrect.

Its Light is within you,
here in your living body;
drink deeply from the heart of its cup
for the Love overflows!

SELF-REALIZATION

One's deep-seeded solitary journey
fatefully shapes a living crucible
whose breath breathes in
the alchemical flame
of Eternal Love
and awakens
The Self.

GIFTS OF LIGHT

The Light
birthed new life
into that Silent Night…
Reflection, Rebirth, Resurrection!
Humanity's eternal gifts
to be opened here on Earth
while in this body where
the *Light* is!

A MACROCOSM

There is a vastness pulsating
in this vesseled vault of flesh!
Boundless and liberated
from self-controlled direction,
soul delights of cosmic play
ensue in this expansive space.

The Creatrix creating in a timeless void
sounds no separateness in
The Song of Her Creation.
"All within all"
explodes the womb
of Great Mystery!

Fire, water, earth, and air…
elementals echo throughout the ages
interweaving, intermingling,
infinitely recycling in
birthing,
creating,
destroying,
intoning a truth incarnate:

*There is a Macrocosm pulsating
in this vesseled vault of flesh!*

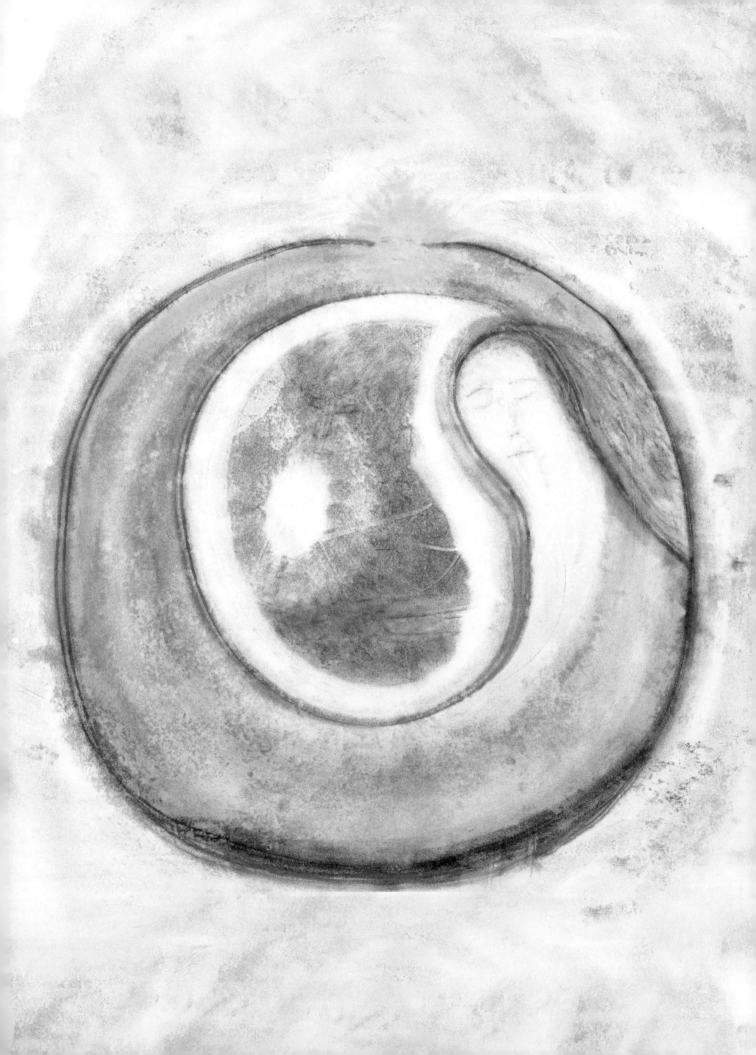

STOP!

Stop searching, stop questioning,
stop wanting to feel good,
to be better, to do it right.
Let these rocks go down the drain.

Stop and realize
who it is you are becoming,
and just be
Who it is you are.

Hafiz* says:
*"I will surrender myself to
Who you keep saying
I Am."*

* Great Sufi Master

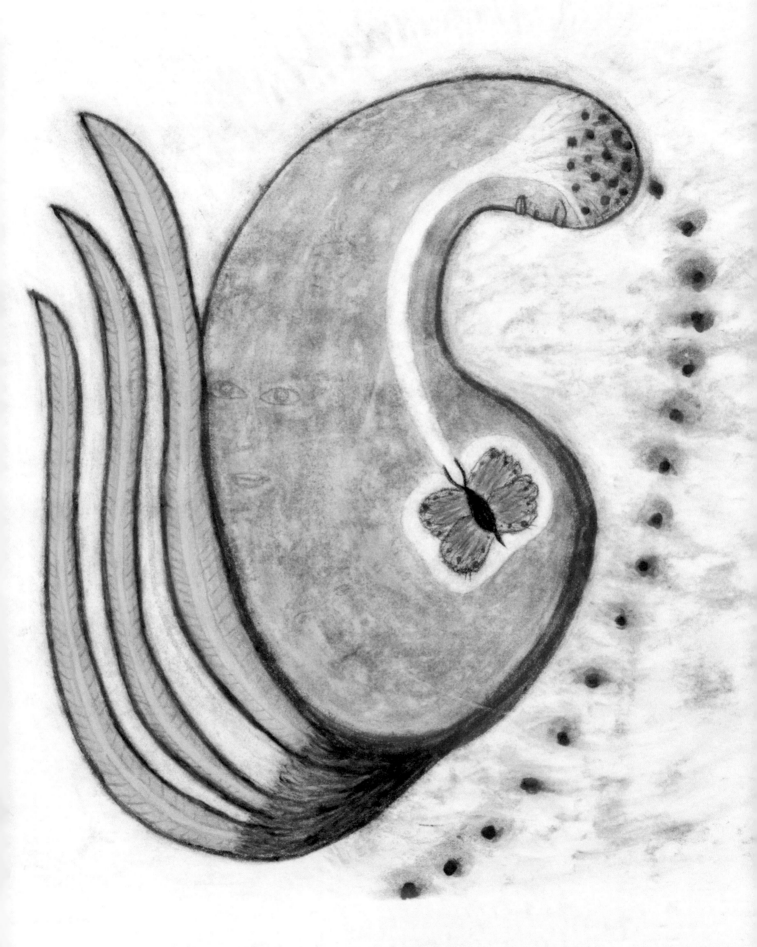

AN ABSOLUTE PRESENCE

There is an absolute Presence
permeating this abode…
a Presence so subtly saturating
infuses the secret depths of soul
and codes the marrowy flesh of bone.

In one silent moment
when you sit in its utter stillness,
this *Absolute Presence*
defines
Who you are.

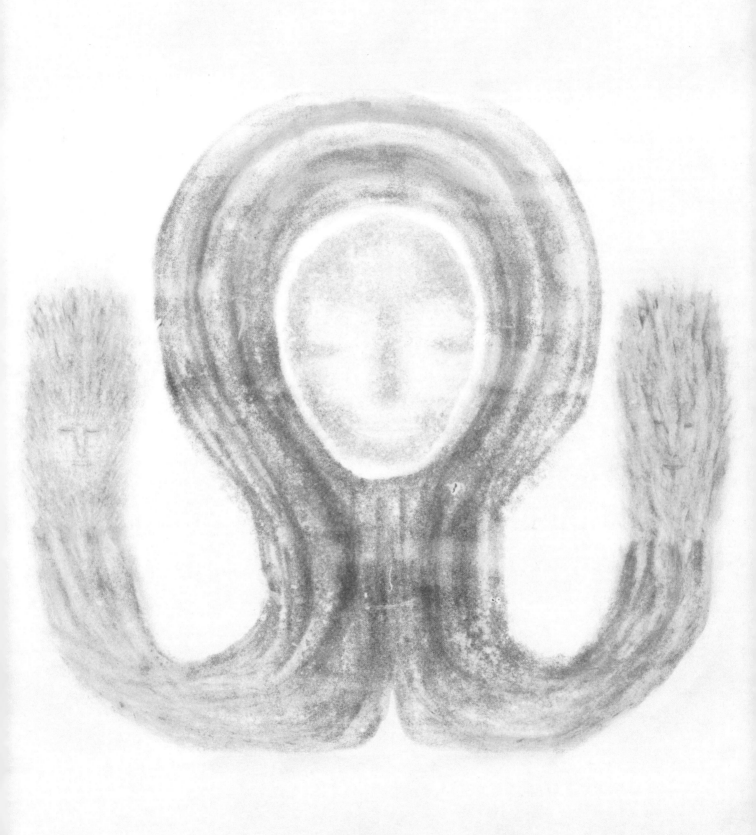

NO DIFFERENCE

I AM – YOU ARE
the Lotus
and the Jewel,
the Dweller
and the Dwelling,
the Phoenix
and the Ash.

I AM - YOU ARE
the Drop
and the Ocean,
the Vision
and the Eye,
the Cup
and the Wine.

I AM - YOU ARE
the Love,
Lover,
and
the Beloved.

I AM - YOU ARE
no difference!

I AM

I AM!
Such profound solemnity
in the bowel of these words!
A marvel of man's existence
expresses his eternal capacity
while be-ing on the Earth.

I AM!
Such innate simplicity
beneath the complexities of life!
A self-abundance so inherently rich
casts aside its costly baggage:
"I want…I do…I need."

I AM!
Such celestial purity
in the pronouncement of these words!
A sacred sound whose utterance
intones the very breadth and depth
of humanity's divinity.

I AM!
What a saturating Presence
sustains this embodied state!

CHRISTED

No privileged dogma here,
instead…
a divine birthright.
Its signature, a template of Light
blueprinting the essence
of every living man.

In the template:
A higher Consciousness descends
paradoxically initiating an ascent
from the solitary soul depths
of every living man.

In the template:
A transcendent path appears
immanently merging the separateness
that courses wild in the mind
of every living man.

In the template:
A compassionate heart forgives
unconditionally freeing conditioned love
locked within the karmic cells
of every living man.

In the template:
no privileged dogma here,
instead…
The Eternal Light
choosing to live
as every living man!

THE TREE OF LIFE

Oh! Symbolic mystical
Kab-ba-`lah!
Rooted in the heavens,
you tell of humanity's divinity
from the glory of ancient times.

Oh! Symbolic mystical
Kab-ba-`lah!
Through four worlds of cosmic truth,
you form the eternal universe
in the fleshened core of man.

Oh! Symbolic mystical
Kab-ba-`lah!
With a wooded design so intricate,
you uphold in synchronous balance
ten spheres of Nothingness.

Oh! Symbolic mystical
Kab-ba-`lah!
Descending, ascending, creating,
entwining, evolving, emanating
man, nature, and divinity
as One.

Oh! Symbolic mystical
Kab-ba-`lah!
Behold your mystery!
Hu-*man*-ity
is
The Tree of Light!

DIVINE DIGNITY

What divine dignity
beholds the creation of man!
Hallowed into being
"of the image and likeness"
royalty descends
and earthened forms become the Kingdom.

What divine dignity
cloaks these inhabitants!
Honored with the solemn gesture
of a passing nod,
living souls embrace
in a mirrored realm of regal reflection.

What divine dignity
bestows the essence of Man!
Knighted into stately existence
with an inheritance of eternal wealth,
commoners and nobles ascend
and earthened forms become the Kingdom.

THE SOUND

Listen…
What is that resonating so deep within us?
A reverberation of the Big Bang?
the Om?
The sound of Creation creating
in unison, in union?

Listen…
We all are entrained,
re-sounding
the sound
of
the One.

Listen!

CREATIVITY

Creativity…
A divine Energy
so beyond its fruited form.
An innate gift, a relationship,
the core of human expression
in dance with Creator, Self, and Soul.

Creativity…
Selfless talent
from a transcendent place.
Waiting, womb-like, out in the ethers
for its appointed time
of conscious birth.

Creativity…
Passionately perpetuating
co-creatively.
A Creator surprised,
delightfully manifesting in myriad forms
through Her own creations of Love!

REED BEDS

We, *dear Beloved*, are
the hollow
and
the breath.

Play us,
hear your
songs of creation
sing!

THE ABYSS OF GREAT MYSTERY

What serenity
awaits a surrender
into the abyss of Great Mystery!

The mind, reluctant in shedding its
ravenous cloak of questions and answers
and righteous knowing,
subtly quiets
as
the abyss of Great Mystery promises
an innate freedom, a sacred emptiness,
a gifted void of place and space.

The mind silently succumbs,
falling deep into
the abyss
within
its
very own
heart-soul!

EMPTINESS

A hidden dwelling
(devoid of noise amidst the noise)
in unsuspecting suddenness
blossoms the seeded lotus
and gifts the human soul.

How effulgent the eye
of this vacant center,
how vast the encircling
that holds in beckoning silence
life's rapturous existence!

This hidden dwelling
(devoid of things amidst all things)
defines its nothingness as everything
and seals its secrets
in an earthened form.

How Infinite the finite
who shapes this holy shrine,
how destined by design
this solid state and living space
of *Emptiness* in man!

BEYOND DETACHMENT

In this state of letting go
beyond detachment
one finds a profound willingness,
a deepening desire wallowing up inside
to allow the death of the forms
that formed the selves' identities.

In detachment,
forms live on "unattached".
In this state of letting go
beyond detachment
nothing remains anymore
to detach from.
The forms themselves fall away
and suddenly, subtly
one finds oneself
living here in formlessness
beyond detachment!

SACRED PRODIGY

We are the celibate Creator
made manifest,
the humanity of a creation
through whom the Creatrix gives birth.

We are the incarnate Word
made flesh,
the daughters and sons
of the most High.

We are the holy Spirit
made eternal,
the immanent descent of
a transcendent Being.

We are the
sacred prodigy
of a
Mystical Love!

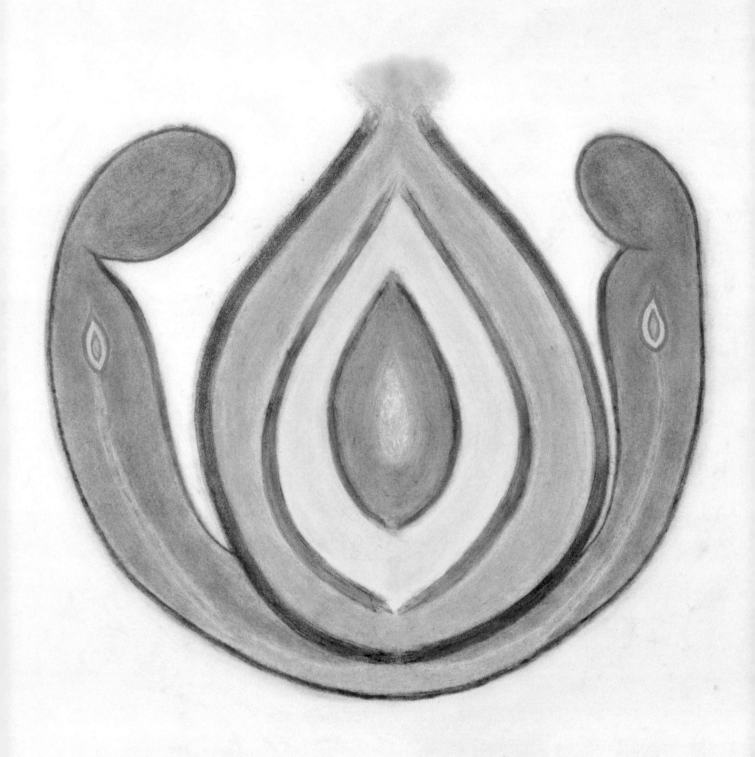

ANANDA'S CUP

Drink of its bliss…
a drunken consciousness of
joy,
delight,
beauty,
existence!

The nectar of a transformed heart,
a divine nourishment of living life,
the elixir of Spirit.

Drink deliciously…
this Bliss is within!

THIS MADONNA AND THE CHILD

One silent Christmas morn
amidst the mystical strains of Josquin's
Missa De Beata Virgine,*
a stunning and deep revelation:

I am this Madonna and the Child,
the star, the stable,
the birther and the birth.
I am all that this Holy Night is,
no need to look afar
only within.

I am this Madonna and the Child,
the ageless ones of Isis and Horus,
Devake and Krishna, Mary and Jesus.
They become now a living reflection
and not separate from
Who I am, Who we all are.

We are the Divine human,
the birther and the birth.
We are
This Madonna and the Child.

* Mass of the Blessed Virgin

61

BODHISATTVA

A pleading prayer for the suffering ones
calls out to the Bodhisattva asking Her bestowal
of mercy and compassion upon them.
And in this calling out
there comes an answer:
*"**You** are this mercy
and
compassionate love!"*

THE TAO

We are *The Tao*…
the everything, the nothing,
the dream - the reality,
the human - the divine,
the fullness and the emptiness.

This coalescing of paradox becomes
a place of no paradox, no distinction
as the self, living out an existence
by Co-existing to become non-existent
becomes *The Tao!*

NOTHING MORE

When one has the courage to say
"There is nothing more to say"
it is at that moment
Love becomes the Reality…
the Essence, Movement, Existence.
It is at that moment
one becomes the only Truth there is.

"There is nothing more to say."

GLOSSARY OF SPIRITUAL MEANINGS & SYMBOLS

Absolute – the One and the innumerable Many; the transcendent and universal Godhead.

Ananda – spiritual delight, ecstasy; Divine Bliss.

Androgynous – a spiritual marriage of the male and female qualities within an individual.

Attachment – connected by feelings of possession to a desire, another, a place, object or situation.

Awakening – a sudden or gradual shift in consciousness opening one to their true and eternal Self.

Being – our divine essence; the soul; the eternal Self; the Divine.

Bird – symbol of the soul; the Holy Spirit in the Christian religion.

Bodhisattva – in Buddhist teachings, a compassionate being who vows to rebirth again and again for the liberation of all beings rather than attain Buddhahood enlightenment just for one's self.

Circle – an ancient and universal symbol of unity, wholeness, and infinity.

Conscious Evolution – a trajectory of human evolution from unconscious to conscious choice.

Consciousness – an awareness within one's self ranging from the mundane to the Divine.

Cosmogenesis – a recent discovery of the sequential evolution of the universe.

Creatrix – a Goddess who creates.

Crucible – a vessel in which substances are heated to high temperatures; a severe trial or test.

Detachment – releasing attachment to a desire, another, a place, object or situation.

Desert – symbol for the quiet; barren yet fruitful.

Diamond Sutra – in Buddhism, the Diamond Sutra is a teaching on nonattachment; a symbol of light.

Divine – the Essence dwelling in all that is; the Nature to be uncovered within one's self.

Emptiness – in Buddhism, the ultimate nature of reality; not possessing an *independent* reality within that defines one's essence; matter not existing in the way we suppose it does.

Enso – Zen circles of enlightenment; a sacred Zen-inspired painting of the ineffable.

Four Worlds of Cosmic Truth – in Judaism, a complete world view manifested in the Divine and human realms whose inspiration comes from the prophet Isaiah.

Grail – symbolized in Arthurian literature as a cup endowed with special powers; a Holy Chalice.

Hafiz – a great Sufi Master and beloved poet of Persia (1320-1389).

I Am – a mystical statement of Divine Presence; All in all; a name for God.

Infinity Sign – an abstract concept describing something without any limit symbolized by the Figure 8 and commonly known as "endless love".

Kabbalah – mystical knowledge and teachings in Judaism believed to have come from God.

Light – symbolic of Truth, Knowledge, and Consciousness.

Lotus – a plant that grows in muddy water and symbolizes the unfolding of a higher consciousness.

Macrocosm – an entire complex structure.

Nothingness – in Asian philosophy, an understanding that ultimate reality is Emptiness or Nothingness; no-thing.

Om (Aum) – a sacred syllable whose sound is said to be the "hum" of the Universe; the sound of Creation.

Phoenix – a mythical bird of great beauty symbolic of rebirth.

Rabia (al-Adawiyya) – female Muslim saint and Sufi mystic (A.D. 713/717 – A.D. 801).

Rainer Maria Wilke – renowned male Bohemian-Austrian poet/novelist (1875-1926).

Reed – the straight stalk of various tall grasses; a wind instrument made from these stalks.

Rose – a flower symbolic of the unfolding of the soul, mystical union, and love.

Self – the true and essential Nature hidden in all beings; the Higher Self.

Soul – the spiritual principle of life separable from the body.

Tao – the flow of life; the Way; "The Tao that can be told is not the eternal Tao." (Lao Tsu)

Tara – a female Goddess (Bohdisattva) associated with Tibetan Buddhism; "Mother of Liberation".

Ten Spheres of Nothingness – Divine attributes that compose the Judaic Tree of Life.

Touch Drawing – a simple process of drawing with one's fingertips on paper placed over paint; a practice of creative, psychological, and spiritual integration. (www.touchdrawing.com)

Tree of Life – in Judaism, the Tree is the source of life and immortality.

Yin-Yang – in Chinese philosophy, the symbol of opposing forces being complementary and giving rise to each other as they interrelate to one another.

SELECT SOURCES

Aurobindo, Sri. *The Life Divine*. Wisconsin: Lotus Press, 2006.

Fox, Matthew. *Illuminations of Hildegard of Bingen*. New Mexico: Bear & Company, Inc., 2002, pg. 44.

Hafiz. *The Gift: Poems by Hafiz*. Translated by Daniel Ladinsky. New York: Penguin Compass, 1999, pg. 323.

Jasper, David. *The Sacred Desert*. Massachusetts: Blackwell Publishing, 2004, pg. 82.

Sakkakini, Wadel El. *First Among Sufis*. Translated by Dr. Nabil Safwat. London: Octagon Press, 1982, pg. 57.

Printed in the United States
By Bookmasters